CONTENTS

1A

Hi, I'm a Bear

Learn

Words

Ⓐ Listen and repeat. Then chant. ▶ 🎧03 🎧04

Ⓑ Listen and repeat. ▶ 🎧05

Ⓒ Stick and say.

Hi, I'm a bear.

1 snake

2 bear

3 fox

4 hippo

5 zebra

6 tiger

7 monkey

Hello, I'm a lion.

8 lion

Quiz

Listen, find, and draw. 🎧 06

1 ◯ **2** △ **3** ☐

Let's Listen

A Listen and sing. Then match. ▶ 🎧07

Hi, Animals!

Hi! Hi! I'm a zebra.

Hello! Hello! I'm a lion.

Hi! Hi! I'm a bear.

Hello! Hello! I'm a monkey.

B Listen and stick. 🎧08

1   2   3   4

Let's Talk

A Listen and number. Then say. 🎧 09

Hello!
I'm a _____.

monkey ◯

snake ◯

lion ◯

fox ◯

tiger ◯

zebra ◯

tiger ◯

hippo ◯

Words

A Match and trace.

1   snake

2       lion

3    fox

4    bear

5    tiger

6   hippo

7    zebra

8      monkey

Subject Link

bear   hippo
monkey   zebra

Ⓐ Stick and write.

1 Sticker

I'm a _____.

2 Sticker

I'm a _____.

3 Sticker

I'm a _____.

4 Sticker

I'm a _____.

Ⓑ Draw your face. Then write your name.

Hello!
I'm _____.

Hi! I'm Jane.

Check-Up

A Listen and choose. 🎧10

1
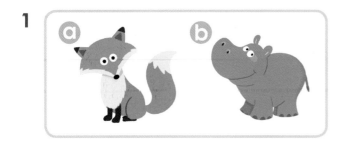

2

3

4

B Listen and number. 🎧11

tiger	bear	hippo	monkey
◯	◯	◯	◯

C Listen and choose. Then say. 🎧12

1

2

A Listen, say, and write. 🎧13

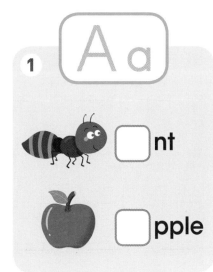

1 Aa
- ☐nt
- ☐pple

2 Bb
- ☐ear
- ☐all

3 Cc
- ☐at
- ☐up

B Listen, circle, and match. 🎧14

1 A B C
a

2 A B C
b

3 A B C
c

C Circle and write.

1
a b c
_____up

2

a b c
_____nt

3
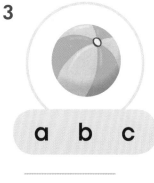
a b c
_____all

UNIT 2 What's This?

Learn

Words

A Listen and repeat. Then chant. ▶ 16 17

B Listen and repeat. ▶ 18

C Stick and say.

> What's this?

 1 kite

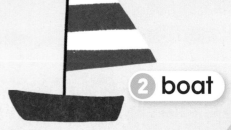 **2** boat

 **3** robot

 **4** drum

It's a kite.

⑥ balloon

⑤ doll

⑦ yo-yo

⑧ top

Quiz

Listen, find, and draw. 🎧19

❶ ◯   ❷ △   ❸ ▢

Let's Listen

A Listen and sing. Then match. ▶ 🎧20

What's This?

What's this?   It's a drum.

What's this?   It's a yo-yo.

What's this?   It's a boat.

What's this?   It's a robot.

B Listen and number. 🎧21

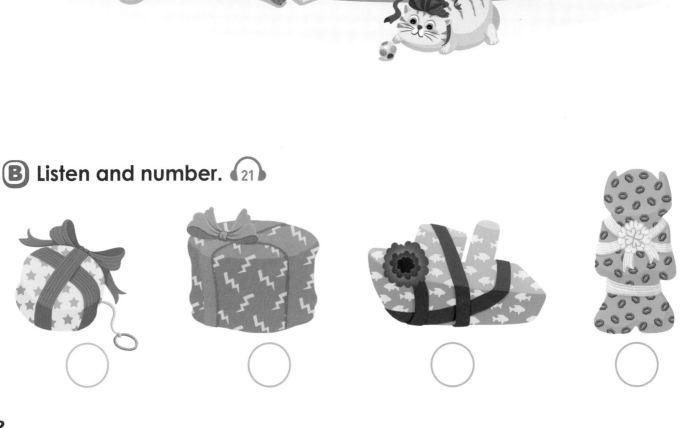

○   ○   ○   ○

Let's Talk

A Listen and stick. Then ask and answer. 🎧22

What's this?

It's a _____.

1. doll
2. yo-yo
3. robot
4. kite
5. top
6. balloon

Words

A Look and write.

doll	drum	robot	kite
top	balloon	boat	yo-yo

1.

2.

3.

4.

5.

6.

7.

8.

Subject Link

boat   doll
drum   yo-yo

A Match and write.

What's This?

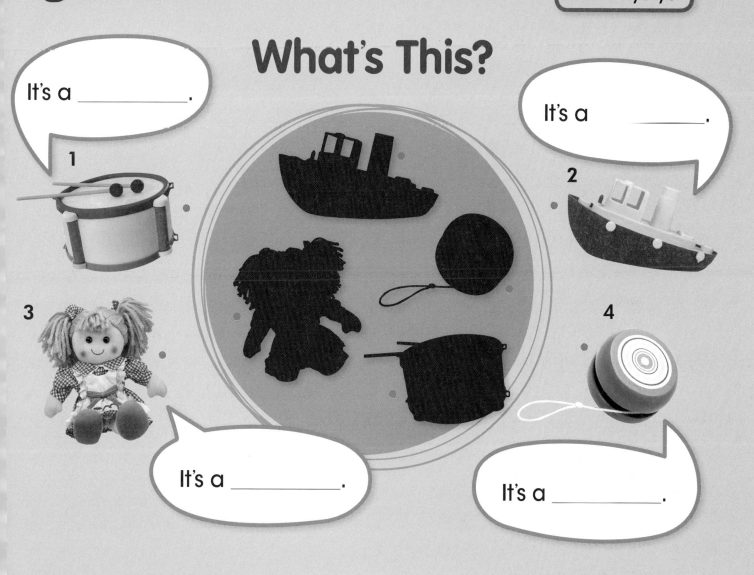

It's a _____.

1

It's a _____.

2

3

It's a _____.

4

It's a _____.

B Find, circle, and write.

What's this?

It's a _____.

A Listen and number. 🎧 23

B Listen and circle. 🎧 24

1	top	balloon
2	yo-yo	drum
3	robot	doll
4	boat	kite

C Listen and choose. Then ask and answer. 🎧 25

1

ⓐ ⓑ

2

ⓐ ⓑ

Ⓐ Listen, say, and write. 🎧 26

1 D d

☐ oll

☐ uck

2 E e
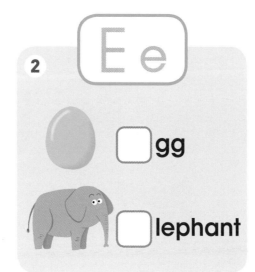
☐ gg

☐ lephant

3 F f
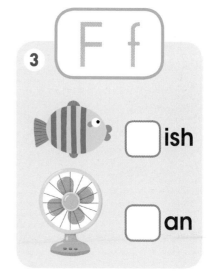
☐ ish

☐ an

Ⓑ Listen and circle. 🎧 27

1

D	E	F
e	d	f

2

E	F	D
d	f	e

3

F	D	E
f	e	d

Ⓒ Match and write.

1

•   E •   • f •   • an

2

•   D •   • e •   • oll

3

•   F •   • d •   • gg

Ⓐ Listen and number. 🎧28

B Read and check.

What's this?

1

☐ Hi, I'm a fox.
☐ Hi, I'm a tiger.

2

☐ It's a robot.
☐ It's a balloon.

3

☐ Hello, I'm a bear.
☐ Hello, I'm a hippo.

4

☐ It's a drum.
☐ It's a yo-yo.

5

☐ Hi, I'm a zebra.
☐ Hello, I'm a snake.

6

☐ It's a top.
☐ It's a boat.

Let's Count

Learn

Words

A Listen and repeat. Then chant. ▶ 🎧30 🎧31

B Listen and repeat. ▶ 🎧32

C Stick and say.

Let's count.

| 1 one |
| 2 two |
| 3 three |
| 4 four |
| 5 five |

6 six

7 seven

8 eight

9 nine

10 ten

Quiz

Listen, find, and draw. 🎧 33

1 ◯ 2 △ 3 ☐

Let's Listen

A Listen and sing. Then count. ▶ 🎧34

Let's Count

Let's count. Let's count.

One! Two! Three!

Four! Five! Six!

Seven! Eight! Nine! Ten!

B Listen and stick. 🎧35

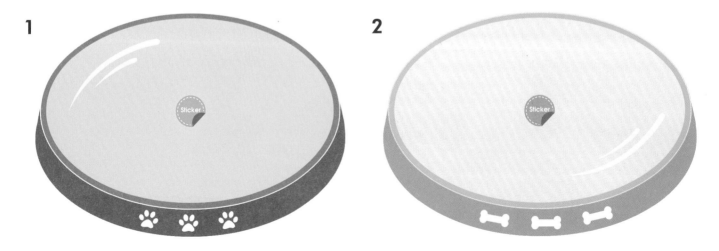

1

2

22

Let's Talk

A Listen, count, and circle. Then say. 🎧 36

five

seven

three

Let's count.

eight

ten

two

Words

A Count, choose, and trace.

1		one
		ten

2		five
		six

3		eight
		two

4	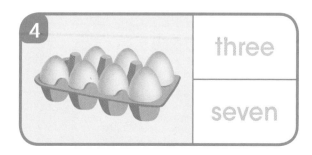	three
		seven

5	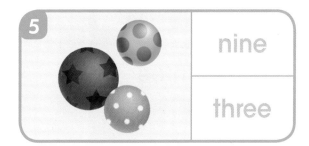	nine
		three

6		eight
		six

7		four
		seven

8		nine
		one

9		five
		two

10		four
		ten

four	eight
six	ten	two

A Count the legs. Then write.

How Many?

1. _____ legs.

2. _____ legs.

3. _____ legs.

4. _____ legs.

5. _____ legs.

B Connect and count the legs. Then write.

Let's count.

_____ legs.

Check-Up

A Listen and circle. 🎧 37

1

2

3

4

B Listen and match. 🎧 38

 1

 2

 3

 4

two

ten

four

six

C Listen and choose. Then say. 🎧 39

1  a b

2  a b

A Listen, say, and write. 🎧40

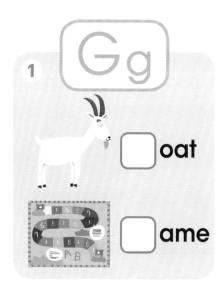

1 Gg
☐ oat
☐ ame

2 Hh
☐ at
☐ ippo

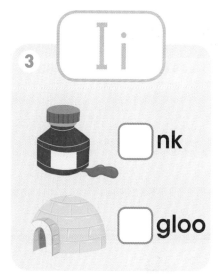

3 Ii
☐ nk
☐ gloo

B Listen and circle. 🎧41

1

Ii	Hh
Gg	Cc

2

Gg	Aa
Hh	Ii

3

Ii	Ff
Gg	Hh

C Match and write.

1  · · G · · h · · _____ at

2  · · I · · g · · _____ gloo

3 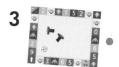 · · H · · i · · _____ ame

UNIT 4 What Color Is It?

Learn

Words

A) Listen and repeat. Then chant. ▶ 🎧43 🎧44

B) Listen and repeat. ▶ 🎧45

C) Stick and say.

1 red

What color is it?

2 blue

3 green

It's yellow.

4 yellow

blue

green

yellow

red

28

5 purple

6 orange

7 black

8 white

orange

purple

black

white

Quiz

Listen, find, and draw. 🎧 46

① ◯   ② △   ③ ▢

Let's Listen

A Listen and sing. Then match.

What Color Is It?

What color is it?   What color is it?

It's red.   It's yellow.

What color is it?   What color is it?

It's blue.   It's green.

B Listen and stick.

1   2   3   4

Sticker   Sticker   Sticker   Sticker

Let's Talk

Listen and number. Then ask and answer. 49

purple ◯

black ◯

white ◯

orange ◯

What color is it?

red ◯

blue ◯

It's _____.

Words

A Trace and check.

1 red
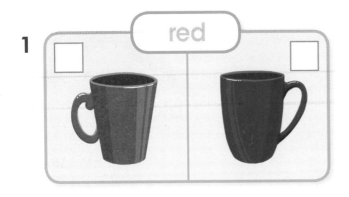

2 blue

3 yellow
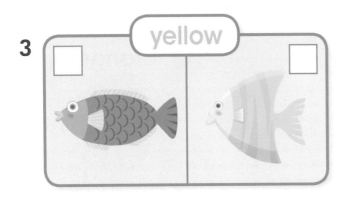

4 green

5 purple

6 orange

7 white

8 black
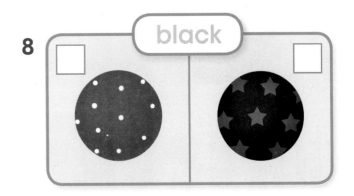

Subject Link

orange   yellow
green   red   blue

A Look and write.

What Color Is It?

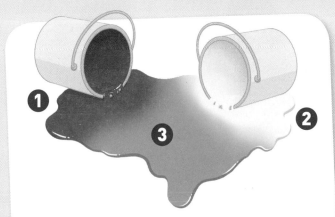

1 It's _____.

2 It's _____.

3 It's _____.

4 It's _____.

5 It's _____.

6 It's _____.

B Color and write.

What color is it?

blue   ?   red

It's _____.

Check-Up

Ⓐ Listen and mark O or X. 🎧50

1   **2**   **3**   **4**

Ⓑ Listen and number. Then match. 🎧51

orange ◯   white ◯   yellow ◯   green ◯

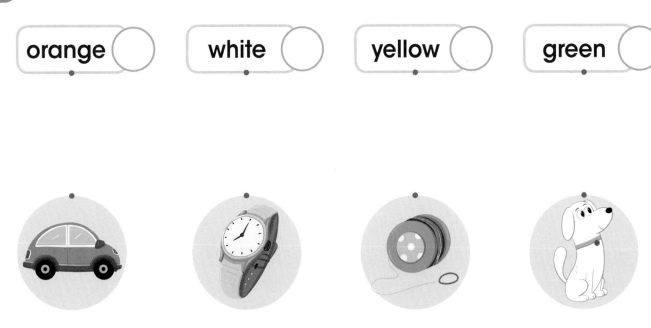

Ⓒ Listen and choose. Then ask and answer. 🎧52

1

ⓐ
ⓑ

2

ⓐ
ⓑ

Phonics

A Listen, say, and write. 🎧 53

1 **Jj**
- ☐ am
- ☐ eep

2 **Kk**
- ☐ ing
- ☐ ite

3 **Ll**
- ☐ emon
- ☐ ion

B Listen, circle, and match. 🎧 54

1 Jj Kk Ll

2 Jj Kk Ll

3 Jj Kk Ll

C Look and write.

1

_____ ion

2

_____ eep

3
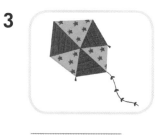

_____ ite

Review 2

A Listen and stick. 🎧 55

36

B Count and circle.

Let's count.

1 (one / four)

2 (five / two)

3 (three / six)

4 (ten / seven)

C Look and match.

What color is it?

1

2

3

4

It's purple.   It's black.   It's yellow.   It's green.

What Shape Is It?

Learn

Words

Ⓐ Listen and repeat. Then chant. ▶ 🎧57 🎧58

Ⓑ Listen and repeat. ▶ 🎧59

Ⓒ Stick and say.

What shape is it?

1 circle

2 heart

3 star

4 square

5 triangle

It's a circle.

6 rectangle

7 diamond

Quiz

Listen, find, and draw.

1 ◯ 2 △ 3 ☐

Unit 5 **39**

Let's Listen

A Listen and sing. Then match.

What Shape Is It?

What shape is it?

It's a circle. It's a heart.

What shape is it?

It's a star. It's a square.

B Listen and stick.

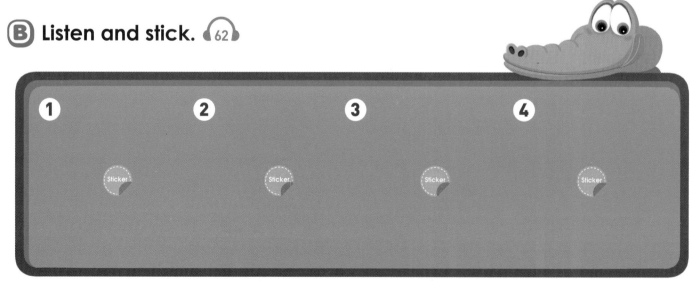

1

2

3

4

Sticker

Sticker

Sticker

Sticker

Let's Talk

A Listen and match. Then ask and answer. 🎧63

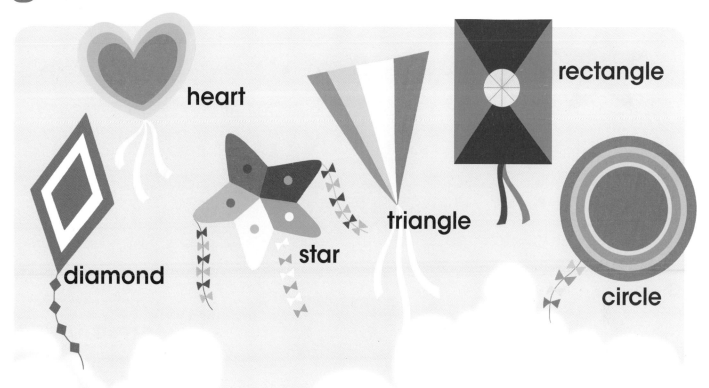

heart

rectangle

diamond

star

triangle

circle

What shape is it?

It's a _____.

Words

(A) Match and trace.

1   circle

2   triangle

3   rectangle

4 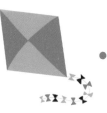  diamond

5   square

6   star

7  square heart

Subject Link

A Write and say.

circle   diamond
square   rectangle

What Shape Is It?

1

It's a _____.

2

It's a _____.

3

It's a _____.

4

It's a _____.

B Circle and write.

What shape is it?

It's a _____.

Check-Up

A Listen and number. 🎧64

B Listen and match. 🎧65

1 •

2 •

3 •

4 •

• star

• square

• diamond

• circle

C Listen and choose. Then ask and answer. 🎧66

1
a
b

2

a
b

44

A Listen, say, and write. 🎧 67

1 **Mm**

☐ oon

☐ onkey

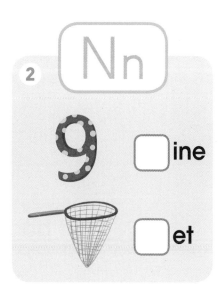

2 **Nn**

☐ ine

☐ et

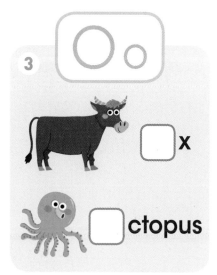

3 **Oo**

☐ x

☐ ctopus

B Listen and circle. 🎧 68

1
M	N	O
o	m	n

2
O	N	M
n	o	m

3
N	M	O
m	o	n

C Look, circle, and write.

1

m n o

_____ oon

2

m n o

_____ et

3

m n o

_____ x

It's a Red Pen

Learn

Words

Ⓐ Listen and repeat. Then chant. ▶ 70 71

Ⓑ Listen and repeat. ▶ 72

Ⓒ Stick and say.

① red **bag**

② red **pen**

It's a bag.

③ yellow **book**

④ yellow **ball**

It's a red bag.

5 blue crayon

6 blue watch

7 green pencil

8 green umbrella

Listen, find, and draw. 🎧 73

1 ◯ **2** △ **3** ☐

Let's Listen

A Listen and sing. Then match. ▶ 🎧74

It's a Green Ball

It's a ball. It's a green ball.

It's a book. It's a purple book.

It's a pen. It's a yellow pen.

It's a crayon. It's a red crayon.

B Listen, number, and color. 🎧75

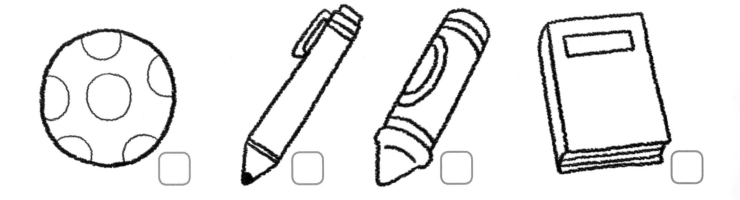

Let's Talk

Listen and stick. Then say. 76

1 red book

2 white ball

3 purple umbrella

4 green pencil

5 blue watch

6 yellow bag

It's a _____ .

Words

A Look and write.

book	ball	pen	pencil
bag	crayon	watch	umbrella

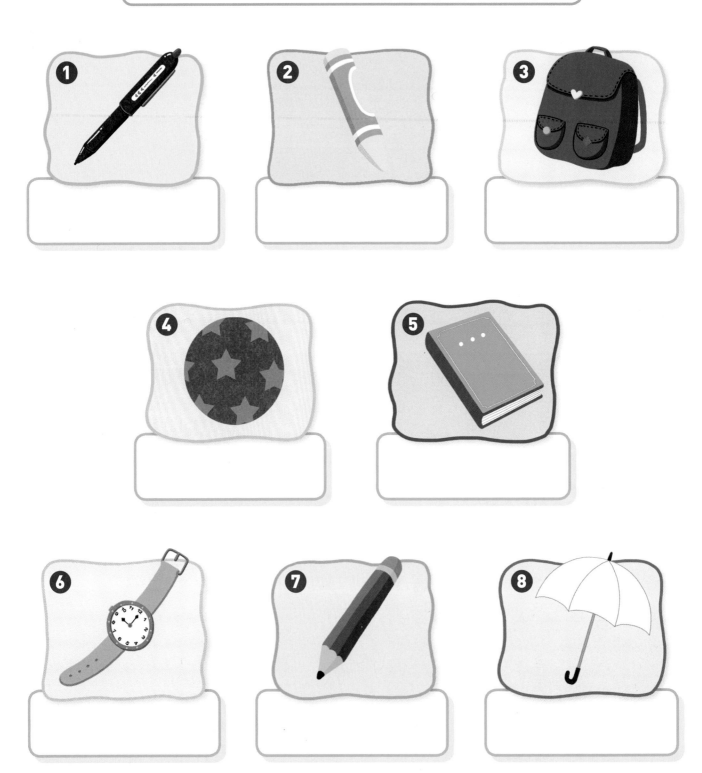

50

Subject Link

umbrella   bag
watch   crayon

Ⓐ Color and write. Then say.

1

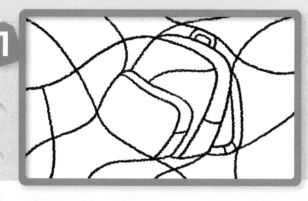

It's a _____ _____.

2

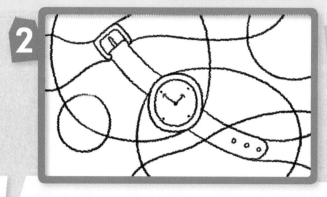

It's a _____ _____.

3

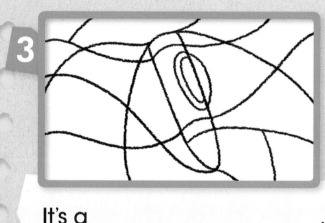

It's a _____ _____.

4

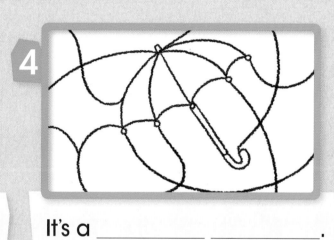

It's a _____ _____.

Ⓑ Find, circle, and write.

It's a purple _____.

Check-Up

A Listen and mark O or X. 🎧77

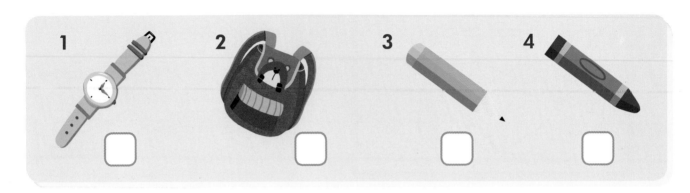

1 2 3 4

B Listen and match. 🎧78

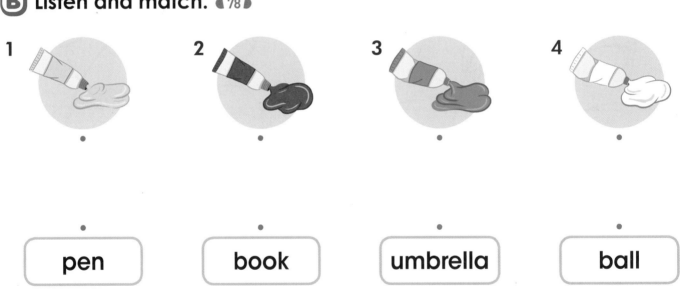

1 2 3 4

pen book umbrella ball

C Listen and choose. Then say. 🎧79

1

ⓐ
ⓑ

2

ⓐ
ⓑ

A Listen, say, and write. 🎧80

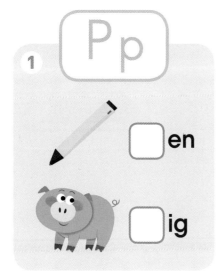

1 Pp
☐ en
☐ ig

2 Qq
☐ ueen
☐ uilt

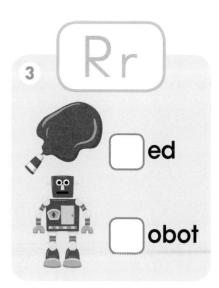

3 Rr
☐ ed
☐ obot

B Listen, circle, and match. 🎧81

1
| P | Q | R |

p

2
| P | Q | R |

q

3
| P | Q | R |

r

C Look and write.

1

_____ueen

2

_____en

3

_____obot

Review 3

Listen and choose. 🎧82

1 ⓐ   ⓑ
2 ⓐ   ⓑ
3 ⓐ   ⓑ
4 ⓐ   ⓑ
5 ⓐ   ⓑ
6 ⓐ   ⓑ
7 ⓐ   ⓑ
8 ⓐ   ⓑ

B Read and circle T or F.

What shape is it?

1
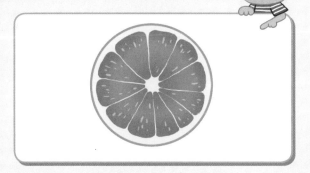
It's a circle. (T / F).

2

It's a blue watch. (T / F).

3

It's a star. (T / F).

4

It's a green book. (T / F).

5

It's a diamond. (T / F).

6

It's a yellow ball. (T / F).

7

It's a rectangle. (T / F).

8

It's a purple umbrella. (T / F).

This Is My Family

Learn

words

(A) Listen and repeat. Then chant. ▶ 🎧84 🎧85

(B) Listen and repeat. ▶ 🎧86

(C) Stick and say.

1 dad

This is my dad.

2 mom

3 sister

4 brother

5 uncle

6 aunt

7 grandpa

8 grandma

Quiz

Listen, find, and draw. 🎧87

1 ◯ 2 △ 3 ☐

Let's Listen

(A) Listen and sing. Then match. ▶ 🎧88

This Is My Family

Hello! Hello!

This is my dad.

This is my mom.

Hello! Hello!

This is my sister.

This is my brother.

(B) Listen and match. 🎧89

1   2   3   4

Let's Talk

mom ◯

uncle ◯

aunt ◯

brother ◯

sister ◯

dad ◯

grandpa ◯

This is my _____.

grandma ◯

Words

A Look and write.

dad　aunt　uncle　grandpa
mom　sister　brother　grandma

me

Subject Link

grandma   mom
grandpa   sister

Ⓐ Look and write.

1 This is my _____.

2 This is my _____.

3 This is my _____.

4 This is my _____.

Ⓑ Draw your family member and introduce.

This is my _____.

Check-Up

A Listen and number. 🎧91

B Listen and mark ○ or ✕. 🎧92

1	2	3	4
mom	uncle	aunt	grandpa
○	○	○	○

C Listen and choose. Then say. 🎧93

1

ⓐ ⓑ

2

ⓐ ⓑ

Ⓐ Listen, say, and write. 🎧94

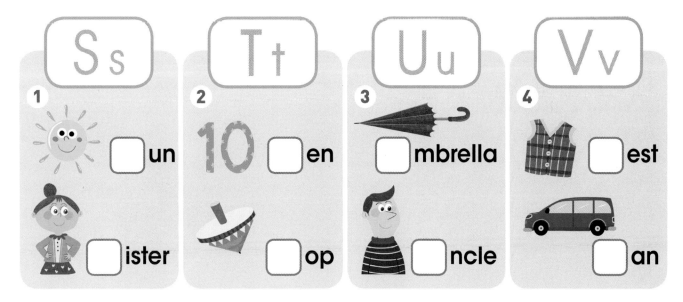

Ss Tt Uu Vv

1
☐un
☐ister

2
☐en
☐op

3
☐mbrella
☐ncle

4
☐est
☐an

Ⓑ Listen and circle. 🎧95

1	
Ss	Dd
Gg	Vv

2	
Tt	Hh
Uu	Mm

3	
Cc	Oo
Uu	Vv

Ⓒ Match and write.

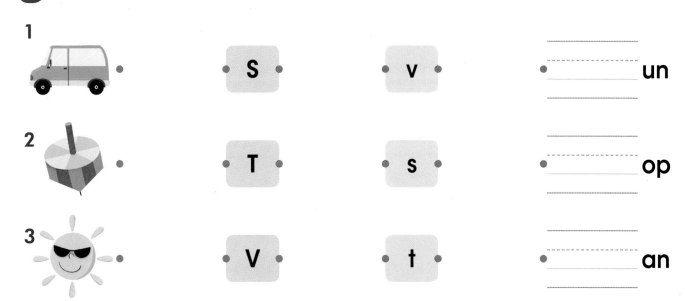

1 • S •   • v •   •_____un

2 • T •   • s •   •_____op

3 • V •   • t •   •_____an

UNIT 8 I Like Cake

Learn

Words

(A) Listen and repeat. Then chant. ▶ 🎧97 🎧98

(B) Listen and repeat. ▶ 🎧99

(C) Stick and say.

I like cake.

1 cake

2 milk

3 cheese

4 bread

5 juice

6 pizza

7 chicken

8 ice cream

Quiz

Listen, find, and draw. 🎧 100

1 ◯   2 △   3 ☐

Let's Listen

I Like Pizza

Pizza! Pizza! I like pizza.

Cheese! Cheese! I like cheese.

Milk! Milk! I like milk.

Ice cream! Ice cream! I like ice cream.

Yum! Yum! Yum!

Ⓑ **Listen and stick.** 🎧102

1

2

3

4

66

Let's Talk

Listen and match. Then say. 103

chicken

juice

ice cream

I like _____.

cake

pizza

bread

Words

Ⓐ Circle and write.

1

cake

chicken

2

milk

ice cream

3

juice

cheese

4

bread

cake

5

pizza

bread

6

milk

juice

7

cheese

chicken

8

ice cream

pizza

Subject Link

milk   cheese
ice cream

A Write and say.

I like _____.

I like _____.

I like _____.

B What do you like? Circle and write.

I like _____.

A Listen and mark ○ or ✗. 104

1   2   3   4

B Listen and match. 105

1   2   3   4

pizza   juice   bread   cake

C Listen and choose. Then say. 106

1

ⓐ

ⓑ

2

ⓐ

ⓑ

A Listen, say, and write. 🎧107

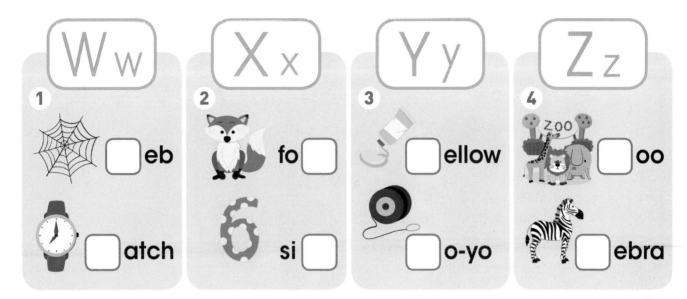

Ww	Xx	Yy	Zz
1 ☐eb	**2** fo☐	**3** ☐ellow	**4** ☐oo
☐atch	si☐	☐o-yo	☐ebra

B Listen, circle, and match. 🎧108

1 | Ww | Xx | Yy |

2 | Zz | Xx | Yy |

3 | Yy | Ww | Zz |

C Circle and write.

1

y   z   x

_____
_____ oo

2

w   y   x

_____
si_____

3

y
z   w   y

_____
_____ ellow

Review 4

(A) Listen and number. 🎧109

(B) Listen and match.

1
2
3
4

72

© **Read and write the letters.**

1 This is my uncle. ☐

2 This is my grandpa. ☐

3 This is my grandma. ☐

4 This is my aunt. ☐

5 I like cheese. ☐

6 I like milk. ☐

7 I like bread. ☐

8 I like juice. ☐

Word List 1A

Unit 1 Hi, I'm a Bear

ant _____

apple _____

ball _____

bear _____

cat _____

cup _____

fox _____

hippo _____

lion _____

monkey _____

snake _____

tiger _____

zebra _____

Unit 2 What's This?

balloon _____

boat _____

doll _____

drum _____

duck _____

egg _____

elephant _____

fan _____

fish _____

kite _____

robot _____

top _____

yo-yo _____

Unit 3 Let's Count

eight _____

five _____

four _____

game _____

goat _____

hat _____

hippo _____

igloo _____

ink _____

nine _____

one _____

seven _____

six _____

ten _____

three _____

two _____

Unit 4 What Color Is It?

black _____

blue _____

green _____

jam _____

jeep _____

king _____

kite _____

lemon _____

lion _____

orange _____

purple _____

red _____

white _____

yellow _____

Unit 5   What Shape Is It?

circle _____

diamond _____

heart _____

monkey _____

moon _____

net _____

nine _____

octopus _____

ox _____

rectangle _____

square _____

star _____

triangle _____

Unit 6   It's a Red Pen

bag _____

ball _____

book _____

crayon _____

pen _____

pencil _____

pig _____

queen _____

quilt _____

red _____

robot _____

umbrella _____

watch _____

Unit 7   This Is My Family

aunt _____

brother _____

dad _____

grandma _____

grandpa _____

mom _____

sister _____

sun _____

ten _____

top _____

umbrella _____

uncle _____

van _____

vest _____

Unit 8   I Like Cake

bread _____

cake _____

cheese _____

chicken _____

fox _____

ice cream _____

juice _____

milk _____

pizza _____

six _____

watch _____

web _____

yellow _____

yo-yo _____

zebra _____

zoo _____

Syllabus 1A

Unit 1 Hi, I'm a Bear

Structure	Vocabulary		Phonics	Subject Link
Hi, I'm a bear.	snake	zebra	Alphabet Sounds	Social Studies
	bear	tiger	Aa, Bb, Cc	
Hello, I'm a lion.	fox	monkey		
	hippo	lion		

Unit 2 What's This?

Structure	Vocabulary		Phonics	Subject Link
What's this?	kite	doll	Alphabet Sounds	Science
It's a kite.	boat	balloon	Dd, Ee, Ff	
	robot	yo-yo		
	drum	top		
Review 1				

Unit 3 Let's Count

Structure	Vocabulary		Phonics	Subject Link
Let's count.	one	six	Alphabet Sounds	Math in Science
	two	seven	Gg, Hh, Ii	
	three	eight		
	four	nine		
	five	ten		

Unit 4 What Color Is It?

Structure	Vocabulary		Phonics	Subject Link
What color is it?	red	purple	Alphabet Sounds	Art
It's yellow.	blue	orange	Jj, Kk, Ll	
	green	black		
	yellow	white		
Review 2				

Unit 5 What Shape Is It?

Structure	Vocabulary		Phonics	Subject Link
What shape is it? It's a circle.	circle heart star square	triangle rectangle diamond	Alphabet Sounds Mm, Nn, Oo	Social Studies

Unit 6 It's a Red Pen

Structure	Vocabulary		Phonics	Subject Link
It's a bag. It's a red bag.	bag pen book ball	crayon watch pencil umbrella	Alphabet Sounds Pp, Qq, Rr	Art
Review 3				

Unit 7 This Is My Family

Structure	Vocabulary		Phonics	Subject Link
This is my dad.	dad mom sister brother	uncle aunt grandpa grandma	Alphabet Sounds Ss, Tt, Uu, Vv	Reading

Unit 8 I Like Cake

Structure	Vocabulary		Phonics	Subject Link
I like cake.	cake milk cheese bread	juice pizza chicken ice cream	Alphabet Sounds Ww, Xx, Yy, Zz	Science
Review 4				

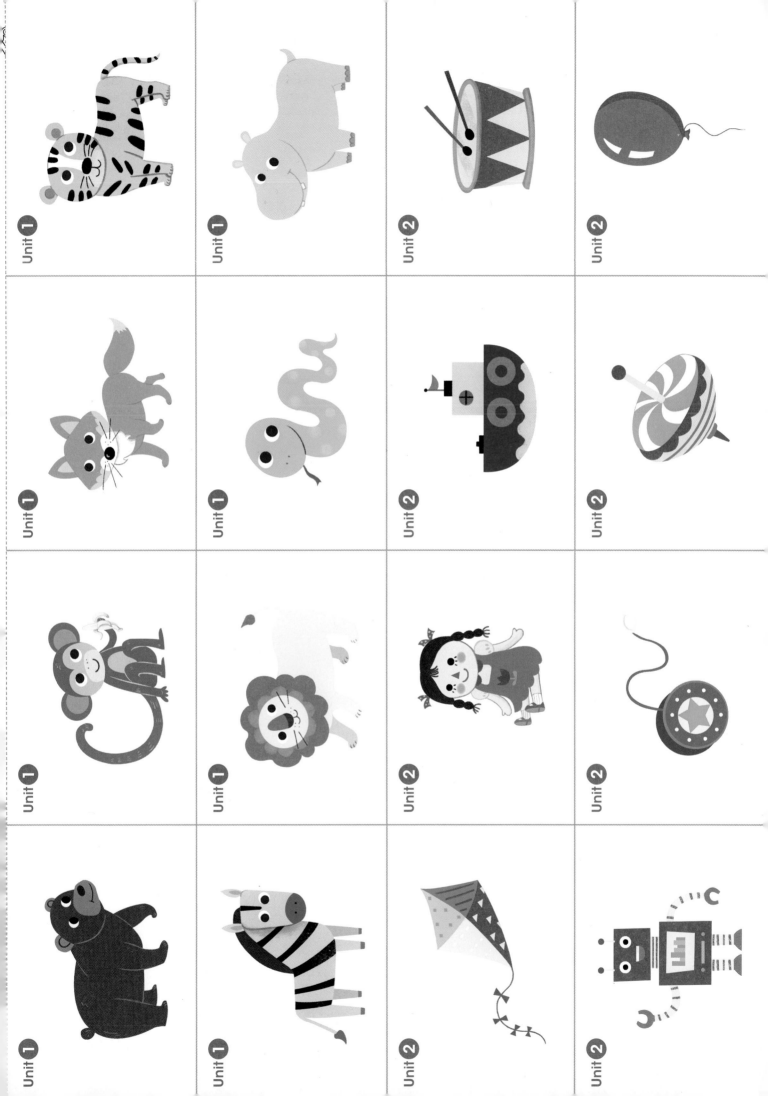

Unit 1

Unit 1

Unit 2

Unit 2

Unit 1

Unit 1

Unit 2

Unit 2

Unit 1

Unit 1

Unit 2

Unit 2

Unit 1

Unit 1

Unit 2

Unit 2

Unit 1 **tiger**	Unit 1 **hippo**	Unit 2 **drum**	Unit 2 **balloon**
Unit 1 **fox**	Unit 1 **snake**	Unit 2 **boat**	Unit 2 **top**
Unit 1 **monkey**	Unit 1 **lion**	Unit 2 **doll**	Unit 2 **yo-yo**
Unit 1 **bear**	Unit 1 **zebra**	Unit 2 **kite**	Unit 2 **robot**

HOW MANY?

ten

six

nine

five

eight

four

seven

three

two

one

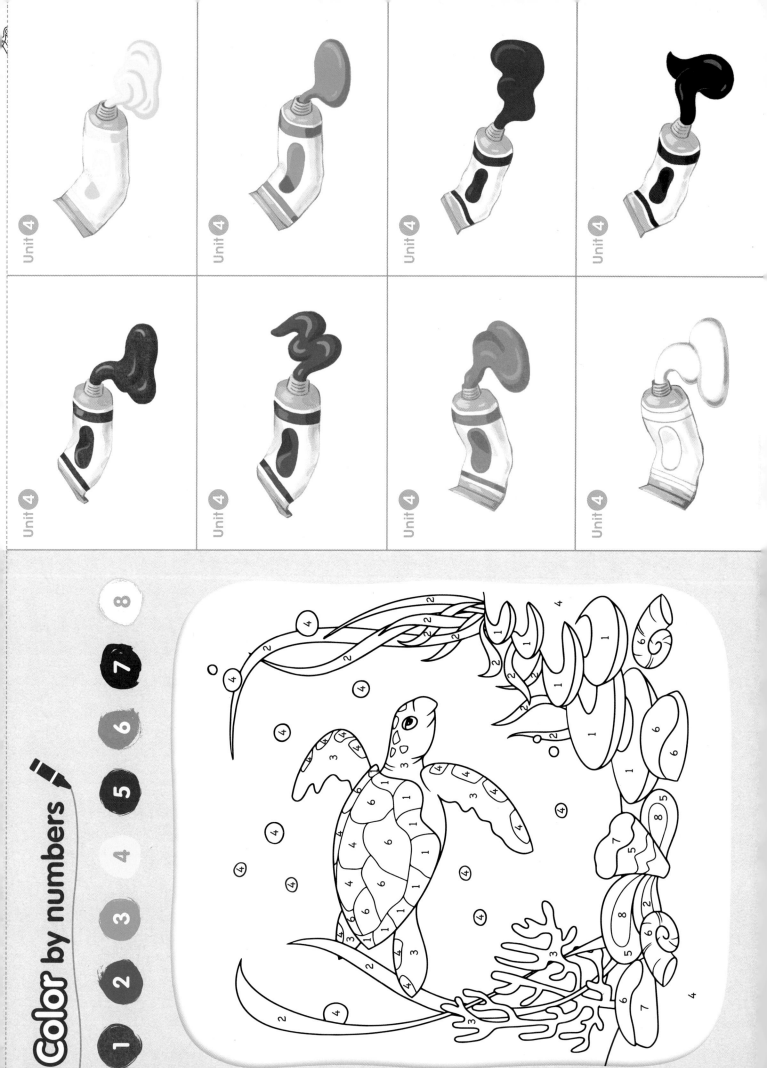

Color by numbers

1 2 3 4 5 6 7 8

yellow

green

purple

black

red

blue

orange

white

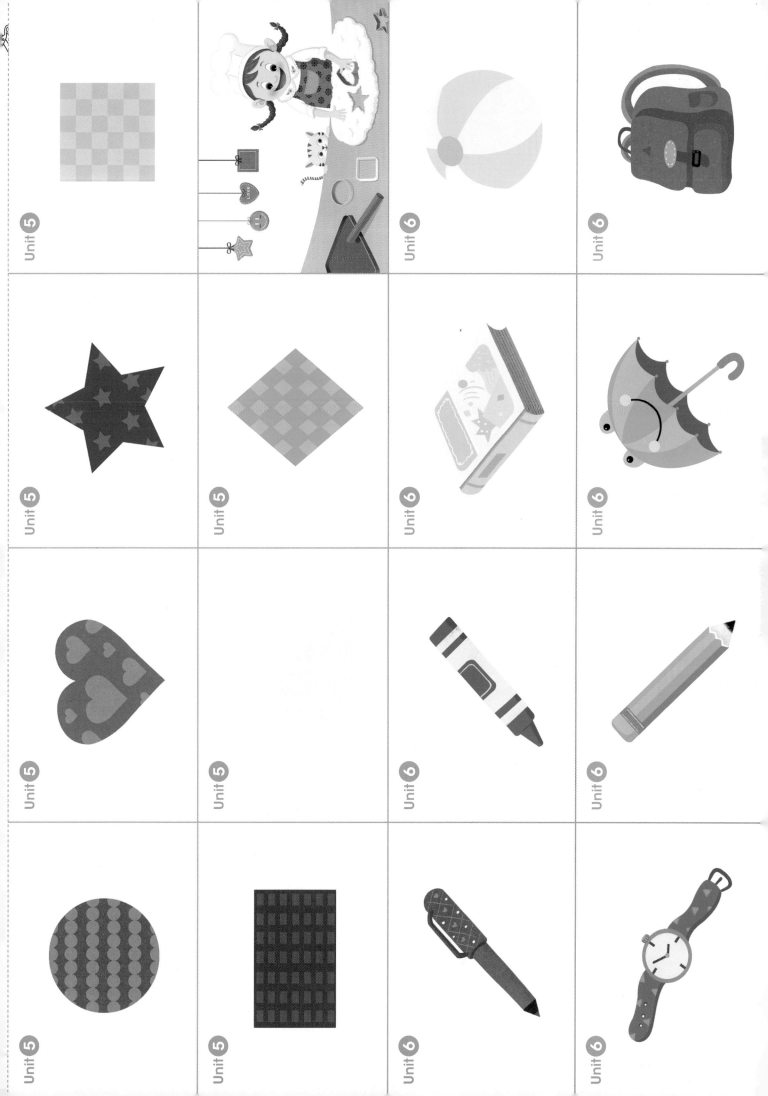

Unit 5

Unit 5

Unit 6

Unit 6

Unit 5

Unit 5

Unit 6

Unit 6

Unit 5

Unit 5

Unit 6

Unit 6

Unit 5

Unit 5

Unit 6

Unit 6

square

What Shape Is It?

ball

bag

star

diamond

book

umbrella

heart

triangle

crayon

pencil

circle

rectangle

pen

watch

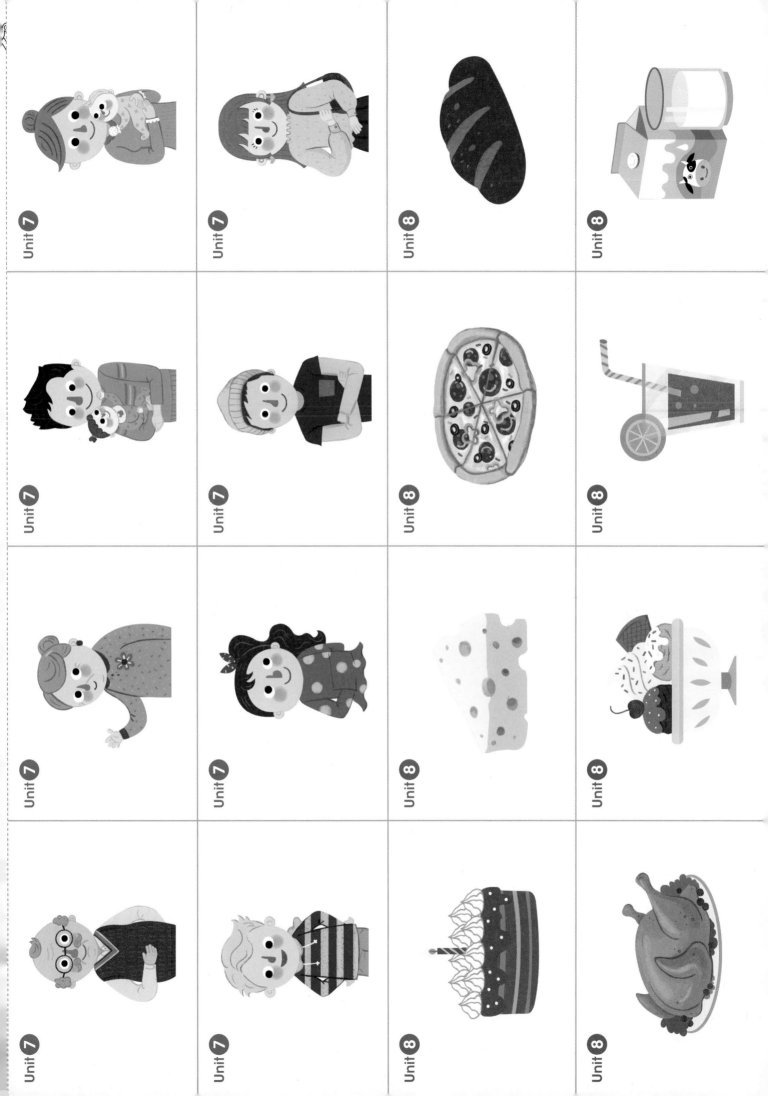

Unit 7

Unit 7

Unit 8

Unit 8

Unit 7

Unit 7

Unit 8

Unit 8

Unit 7

Unit 7

Unit 8

Unit 8

Unit 7

Unit 7

Unit 8

Unit 8

Unit 7	Unit 7	Unit 8	Unit 8
mom	aunt	bread	milk
Unit 7	Unit 7	Unit 8	Unit 8
dad	uncle	pizza	juice
Unit 7	Unit 7	Unit 8	Unit 8
grandma	sister	cheese	ice cream
Unit 7	Unit 7	Unit 8	Unit 8
grandpa	brother	cake	chicken

Phonics

[11-12] Look and choose.
그림을 보고, 주어진 단어와 첫소리가 같은 것을 고르세요.

11

<u>a</u>nt

ⓐ

ⓑ

ⓒ

ⓓ

12

<u>j</u>am

ⓐ

ⓑ

ⓒ

ⓓ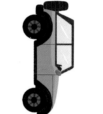

[13-14] Look and choose.
그림을 보고, 알맞은 단어를 고르세요.

13

ⓐ lion   ⓑ fox

ⓒ hippo   ⓓ zebra

14

ⓐ red   ⓑ blue

ⓒ white   ⓓ purple

15 **Look and choose.**
그림을 보고, 빈칸에 알맞은 단어를 고르세요.

It's a _____ .

ⓐ kite   ⓑ boat

ⓒ robot   ⓓ balloon

[16-17] Look and choose.
그림을 보고, 알맞은 것을 고르세요.

16

ⓐ I'm a bear.   ⓑ I'm a lion.

ⓒ I'm a tiger.   ⓓ I'm a monkey.

17

ⓐ It's a drum.   ⓑ It's a top.

ⓒ It's a yo-yo.   ⓓ It's a doll.

[18-19] Look and write.
그림을 보고, 빈칸에 알맞은 말을 써서 대화를 완성하세요.

18

A: What color is it?

B: It's _____ .

19

A: Let's count.

B: One, two, three, four, _____ .

20 **Unscramble.**
단어를 배열하여 알맞은 문장을 만드세요.

(a / I'm / Hello, / snake / .)

_____

Midterm TEST 1A

Institute

Name

Score /100

[1-2] Listen and choose.
잘 듣고, 알맞은 그림을 고르세요.

1
ⓐ
ⓑ
ⓒ
ⓓ

2
ⓐ
ⓑ
ⓒ
ⓓ

3 Listen and choose.
잘 듣고, 그림에 알맞은 것을 고르세요.

ⓐ ⓑ ⓒ ⓓ

Phonics

[4-5] Listen and choose.
잘 듣고, 들려주는 단어들의 공통된 첫소리 글자를 고르세요.

4 ⓐ Bb ⓑ Cc
ⓒ Dd ⓓ Ff

5 ⓐ Gg ⓑ Ii
ⓒ Jj ⓓ Ll

[6-7] Listen and choose.
잘 듣고, 그림에 알맞은 것을 고르세요.

6

ⓐ ⓑ ⓒ ⓓ

7

ⓐ ⓑ ⓒ ⓓ

8 Listen and choose.
잘 듣고, 대화에 알맞은 그림을 고르세요.

ⓐ
ⓑ
ⓒ
ⓓ

9 Listen and choose.
잘 듣고, 빈칸에 알맞은 단어를 고르세요.

Hi, I'm a _____ .

ⓐ bear ⓑ tiger
ⓒ snake ⓓ monkey

10 Listen and choose.
잘 듣고, 빈칸에 알맞은 대답을 고르세요.

A: What color is it?
B: _____

ⓐ ⓑ ⓒ ⓓ

[11-12] Look and choose.
그림을 보고, 그림의 단어와 첫소리가 같은 것을 고르세요.

11

ⓐ nine ⓑ pig

ⓒ mom ⓓ ox

12

ⓐ sun ⓑ web

ⓒ ten ⓓ van

[13-14] Read and mark ○ or X.
다음을 읽고, 그림과 일치하면 ○ 표, 일치하지 않으면 X 표를 하세요.

13

green pencil ☐

14

rectangle ☐

15 Look and choose.
그림을 보고, 빈칸에 알맞은 단어를 고르세요.

I like _____ .

ⓐ bread ⓑ juice

ⓒ pizza ⓓ chicken

16 Look and choose.
그림을 보고, 알맞은 것을 고르세요.

ⓐ This is my dad.

ⓑ This is my uncle.

ⓒ This is my grandma.

ⓓ This is my brother.

17 Look and choose.
그림을 보고, 알맞은 것을 고르세요.

ⓐ I like milk.

ⓑ I like pizza.

ⓒ I like cheese.

ⓓ I like ice cream.

[18-19] Look and complete.
그림을 보고, 빈칸에 알맞은 말을 쓰세요.

18

It's a blue _____ .

19

A: What shape is it?

B: It's a _____ .

20 Unscramble.
단어를 배열하여 알맞은 문장을 만드세요.

(green / a / book / It's / .)

_____ →

Final TEST 1A

Institute

Name

Score   /100

1 Listen and choose.
잘 듣고, 알맞은 그림을 고르세요.

ⓐ   ⓑ

ⓒ    ⓓ

[2-3] Listen and choose.
잘 듣고, 그림에 알맞은 것을 고르세요.

2

ⓐ   ⓑ   ⓒ   ⓓ

3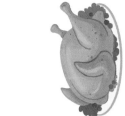

ⓐ   ⓑ   ⓒ   ⓓ

Phonics

[4-5] Listen and choose.
잘 듣고, 첫소리 글자가 일치하지 않는 것을 고르세요.

4 ⓐ Mm   ⓑ Pp
   ⓒ Oo   ⓓ Rr

5 ⓐ Ss   ⓑ Vv
   ⓒ Ww   ⓓ Zz

[6-7] Listen and choose.
잘 듣고, 알맞은 그림을 고르세요.

6 ⓐ   ⓑ

   ⓒ   ⓓ

7 ⓐ    ⓑ

   ⓒ    ⓓ

8 Listen and choose.
잘 듣고, 그림에 알맞은 문장을 고르세요.

ⓐ   ⓑ   ⓒ   ⓓ

9 Listen and choose.
잘 듣고, 빈칸에 알맞은 단어를 고르세요.

This is my _____.

ⓐ dad   ⓑ sister
ⓒ uncle   ⓓ brother

10 Listen and choose.
잘 듣고, 빈칸에 알맞은 대답을 고르세요.

A: What shape is it?
B: _____

ⓐ   ⓑ   ⓒ   ⓓ

Let's Go·1A

Unit **1** pp. 2~3

bear	monkey	fox	tiger
zebra	lion	snake	hippo

p. 4

p. 7

Unit **2** pp. 10~11

kite	robot	boat	drum
doll	yo-yo	top	balloon

p. 13

Unit **3** pp. 20~21

one	two	three	four	five
six	seven	eight	nine	ten

p. 22

blue	red	green	yellow
black	purple	orange	white

p. 30

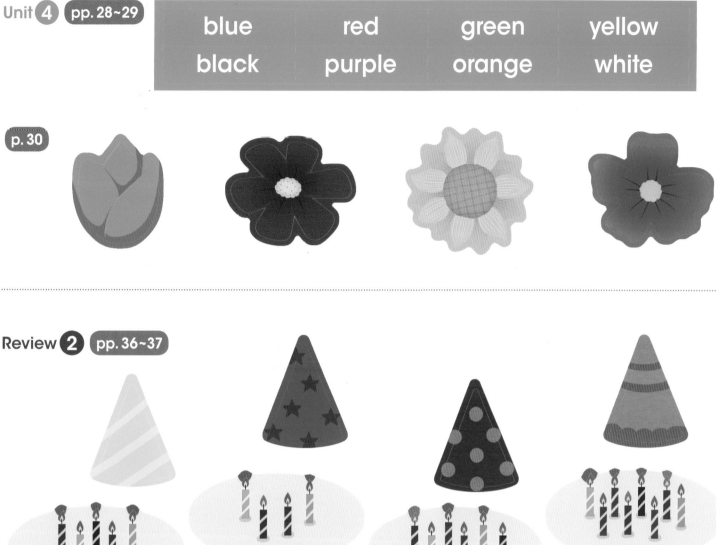

Review **2** pp. 36~37

circle	star	triangle	diamond
heart	square	rectangle	

p. 40

Unit 6 — pp. 46~47

ball	book	crayon	watch
bag	pen	pencil	umbrella

p. 49

Unit 7 — pp. 56~57

grandpa	mom	uncle	brother
grandma	dad	sister	aunt

Unit 8 — pp. 64~65

juice	milk	cheese	chicken
pizza	cake	bread	ice cream

p. 66

2nd Edition

LET'S GO

to the English World

1A

Word Book
& Workbook

CHUNJAE EDUCATION, INC.

2nd Edition

LET'S GO

to the English World

1A

Word Book

(A) **Listen and trace. Then say.** 🎧02

❶
snake
뱀

❷
bear
곰

❸
fox
여우

❹
hippo
하마

❺
zebra
얼룩말

❻
tiger
호랑이

❼
monkey
원숭이

❽
lion
사자

 **Hi, I'm a bear.** 안녕, 나는 곰이야.

 **Hello, I'm a lion.** 안녕, 나는 사자야.

B Trace, write, and say.

❶ 뱀　　　snake

❷ 곰　　　bear

❸ 여우　　fox

❹ 하마　　hippo

❺ 얼룩말　zebra

❻ 호랑이　tiger

❼ 원숭이　monkey

❽ 사자　　lion

What's This?

A Listen and trace. Then say. 🎧15

①
kite
연

②
boat
보트

③
robot
로봇

④
drum
북

⑤
doll
인형

⑥
balloon
풍선

⑦
yo-yo
요요

⑧
top
팽이

What's this? 이것은 무엇이니?

It's a kite. 그것은 연이야.

B Trace, write, and say.

① 연　kite

② 보트　boat

③ 로봇　robot

④ 북　drum

⑤ 인형　doll

⑥ 풍선　balloon

⑦ 요요　yo-yo

⑧ 팽이　top

Let's Count

Ⓐ Listen and trace. Then say. 🎧 29

①  **one**
하나

②  **two**
둘

③  **three**
셋

④  **four**
넷

⑤  **five**
다섯

⑥  **six**
여섯

⑦  **seven**
일곱

⑧  **eight**
여덟

⑨  **nine**
아홉

⑩  **ten**
열

 **Let's count.** 세어 보자.

B Trace, write, and say.

❶ 하나   one

❷ 둘   two

❸ 셋   three

❹ 넷   four

❺ 다섯   five

❻ 여섯   six

❼ 일곱   seven

❽ 여덟   eight

❾ 아홉   nine

❿ 열   ten

What Color Is It?

Ⓐ Listen and trace. Then say. 🎧42

①
red
빨간색

②
blue
파란색

③
green
초록색

④
yellow
노란색

⑤
purple
보라색

⑥
orange
주황색

⑦
black
검은색

⑧
white
흰색

 **What color is it?** 그것은 무슨 색깔이니?

 **It's yellow.** 그것은 노란색이야.

B Trace, write, and say.

① 빨간색   red

② 파란색   blue

③ 초록색   green

④ 노란색   yellow

⑤ 보라색   purple

⑥ 주황색   orange

⑦ 검은색   black

⑧ 흰색   white

UNIT 5 What Shape Is It?

Ⓐ Listen and trace. Then say. 🎧 56

①  **circle**
동그라미

②  **heart**
하트 모양

③  **star**
별 모양

④  **square**
정사각형

⑤  **triangle**
삼각형

⑥  **rectangle**
직사각형

⑦  **diamond**
마름모

 **What shape is it?** 그것은 무슨 모양이니?

 **It's a circle.** 그것은 동그라미야.

B Trace, write, and say.

❶ 동그라미   circle

❷ 하트 모양   heart

❸ 별 모양   star

❹ 정사각형   square

❺ 삼각형   triangle

❻ 직사각형   rectangle

❼ 마름모   diamond

It's a Red Pen

Ⓐ Listen and trace. Then say. 🎧69

①  **bag**
가방

②  **pen**
펜

③  **book**
책

④  **ball**
공

⑤  **crayon**
크레용

⑥  **watch**
손목시계

⑦  **pencil**
연필

⑧  **umbrella**
우산

It's a bag. 그것은 가방이야.
It's a red bag. 그것은 빨간색 가방이야.

Review

red   yellow   blue   green   orange   purple   white   black

B Trace, write, and say.

① 가방   bag

② 펜   pen

③ 책   book

④ 공   ball

⑤ 크레용   crayon

⑥ 손목시계   watch

⑦ 연필   pencil

⑧ 우산   umbrella

This Is My Family

Ⓐ Listen and trace. Then say. 🎧83

①  **dad**
아빠

②  **mom**
엄마

③  **sister**
언니, 누나, 여동생

④  **brother**
오빠, 형, 남동생

⑤  **uncle**
삼촌, 이모부, 고모부

⑥  **aunt**
고모, 이모, 숙모

⑦  **grandpa**
할아버지

⑧  **grandma**
할머니

 **This is my dad.** 이분은 우리 아빠셔.

B Trace, write, and say.

① 아빠   dad

② 엄마   mom

③ 언니, 누나, 여동생   sister

④ 오빠, 형, 남동생   brother

⑤ 삼촌, 이모부, 고모부   uncle

⑥ 고모, 이모, 숙모   aunt

⑦ 할아버지   grandpa

⑧ 할머니   grandma

Ⓐ Listen and trace. Then say. 🎧 96

①  **cake**
케이크

②  **milk**
우유

③  **cheese**
치즈

④  **bread**
빵

⑤  **juice**
주스

⑥  **pizza**
피자

⑦  **chicken**
치킨

⑧  **ice cream**
아이스크림

I like cake. 나는 케이크를 좋아해.

B Trace, write, and say.

1 케이크   cake

2 우유   milk

3 치즈   cheese

4 빵   bread

5 주스   juice

6 피자   pizza

7 치킨   chicken

8 아이스크림   ice cream

Workbook

1A

Hi, I'm a Bear

Learn

A Look and write.

bear	monkey	tiger	snake
zebra	fox	hippo	lion

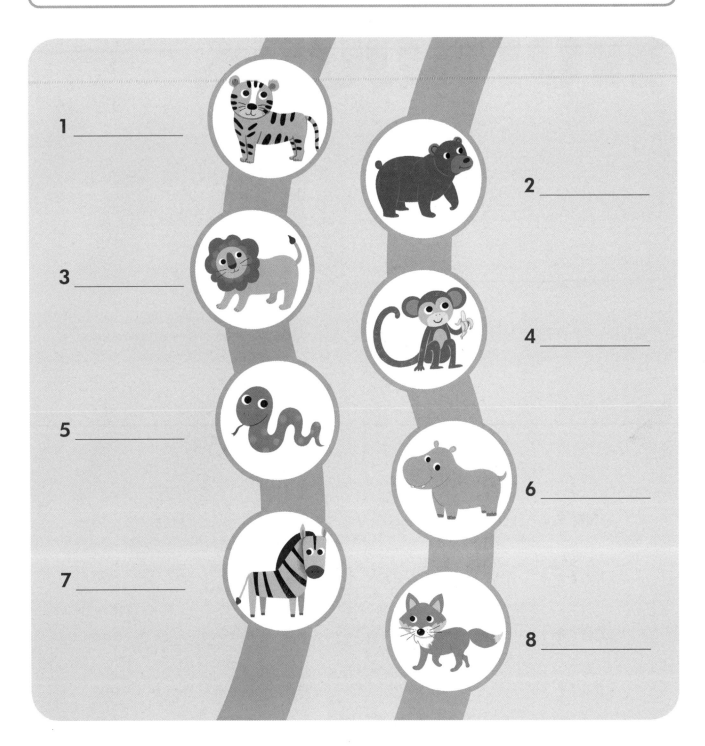

1 _____

2 _____

3 _____

4 _____

5 _____

6 _____

7 _____

8 _____

B Read and match.

1 Hi, I'm a hippo. •

• ⓐ

2 Hi, I'm a tiger. •

• ⓑ

3 Hi, I'm a bear. •

• ⓒ

4 Hello, I'm a monkey. •

• ⓓ

5 Hello, I'm a fox. •

• ⓔ

6 Hello, I'm a zebra. •

• ⓕ

Let's Talk

Ⓐ Circle and write.

1  (lion / tiger)   Hi, I'm a _____.

2  (zebra / fox)   Hi, I'm a _____.

3  (hippo / snake)   Hello, I'm a _____.

4 (monkey / bear)   Hello, I'm a _____.

Ⓑ Read and check.

1

☐ Hi, I'm a bear.

☐ Hi, I'm a snake.

2

☐ Hello, I'm a monkey.

☐ Hello, I'm a hippo.

Words

A Unscramble.

1

e b r a

I'm a _____ .

2

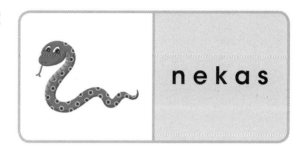

n e k a s

I'm a _____ .

3

x f o

I'm a _____ .

4

o n l i

I'm a _____ .

5

k o n m y e

I'm a _____ .

6

o p h i p

I'm a _____ .

7

r i g t e

I'm a _____ .

8

r z b a e

I'm a _____ .

Subject Link

Ⓐ Read and match.

1   I'm a bear.   •

2   I'm a hippo.   •

3   I'm a monkey.   •

Ⓑ Read and number.

1   I'm a zebra.
2   I'm a lion.
3   I'm a snake.
4   I'm a tiger.

Phonics

A sound words = ○
b sound words = △
c sound words = □

Ⓐ Draw and write.

1
☐ ear

2

☐ at

3
☐ up

4

☐ nt

5
☐ all

6

☐ pple

What's This?

Learn

A Trace and match.

1 kite 2 doll 3 boat 4 balloon

5 top 6 robot 7 drum 8 yo-yo

B Trace and circle.

1 It's a doll.

2 It's a robot.

3 It's a top.

4 It's a kite.

5 It's a yo-yo.

6 It's a drum.

Let's Talk

A Match and write.

1  It's • • a top. • • It's a r_____.

2  It's • • a robot. • • It's a b_____.

3  It's • • a balloon. • • It's a d_____.

4  It's • • a drum. • • It's a t_____.

B Color, read, and check.

1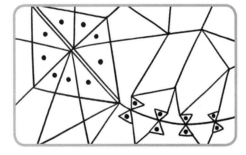

A: What's this?

B: ☐ It's a yo-yo.

☐ It's a kite.

2

A: What's this?

B: ☐ It's a boat.

☐ It's a doll.

Words

(A) Find and circle. Then complete.

c	k	i	t	e	i	d	t
y	o	y	o	r	r	o	o
w	b	o	a	t	o	l	p
d	r	u	m	d	b	l	r
y	b	a	l	l	o	o	n
h	c	n	n	s	t	t	l

1

k __ t __

2

t __ p

3

d __ l __

4

__ oa __

5

d __ __ m

6

__ o-y __

7

r __ bo __

8
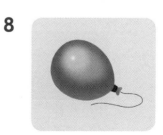
__ al __ o __ n

Subject Link

A Read and circle.

1

A: What's this?

B: It's a (drum / kite).

2

A: What's this?

B: It's a (balloon / boat).

3

A: What's this?

B: It's a (robot / doll).

4

A: What's this?

B: It's a (top / yo-yo).

B Follow and write.

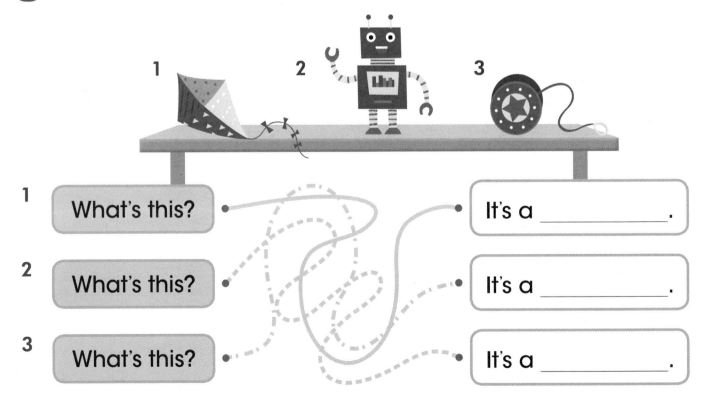

1 What's this?   It's a _____.

2 What's this?   It's a _____.

3 What's this?   It's a _____.

Phonics

Ⓐ Write and circle.

1

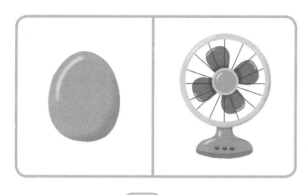

☐ gg

2

☐ ish

3

☐ oll

4

☐ uck

5

☐ an

6

☐ lephant

Let's Count

Learn

A Trace, count, and circle.

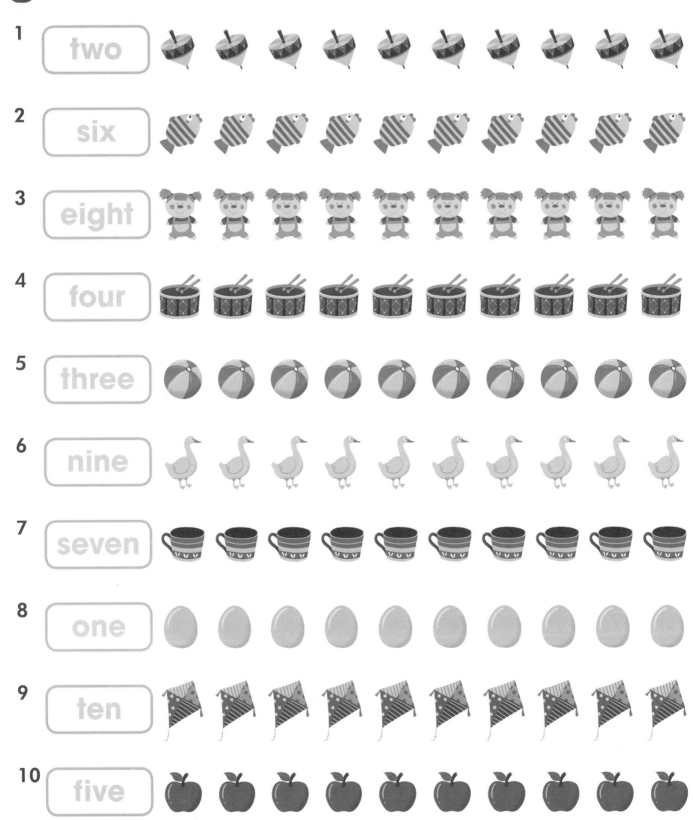

1 two

2 six

3 eight

4 four

5 three

6 nine

7 seven

8 one

9 ten

10 five

B **Count and circle.**

Let's count.

1   one   two   three   four   five

2   one   two   three   four   five

3   one   two   three   four   five

4   six   seven   eight   nine   ten

5   six   seven   eight   nine   ten

Let's Talk

(A) Count, match, and write.

Let's count.

1

o _____ _____

t _____ _____

2

3

f _____ _____ _____

n _____ _____ _____

4

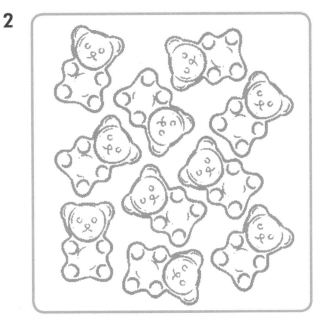

(B) Read and color.

1

Let's count.
One, two, three, four, five.

2

Let's count.
One, two, three, four, five,
six, seven.

34

Words

A Unscramble and write.

1. 7 — veens

2. 3 — rehet

3. 1 — eon

4. 9 — ienn

5. 5 — feiv

6. 4 — ufor

7. 2 — wot

8. 10 — net

9. 6 — xsi

10. 8 — gihet

Subject Link

A **Count the legs and match.**

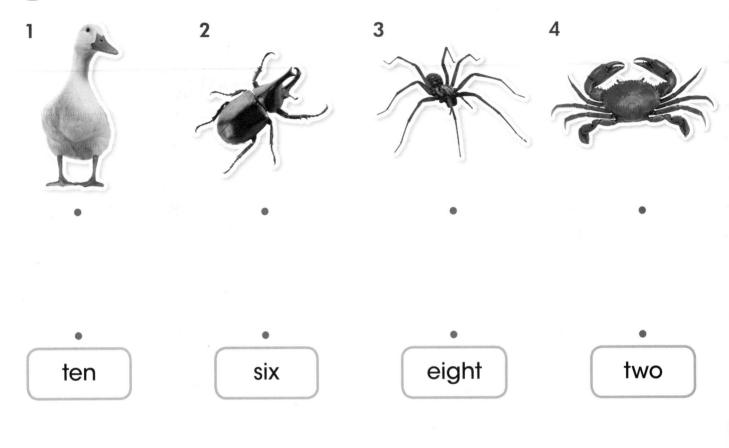

1

2

3

4

| ten | six | eight | two |

B **Read and draw stars.**

1

Let's count.
One, two, three.

2

Let's count.
One, two, three, four, five.

36

Phonics

A Match and write.

1

____at

 g

2

____ame

3

____oat

 h

4

____gloo

5

____nk

 i

6

____ippo

B Look at A. Write the words.

Gg	Hh	Ii
goat		

What Color Is It?

Learn

A Match and write.

1
빨간색
_____

orange •

black •

2
주황색

3
노란색
_____

blue •

red •

4
검은색

5
파란색
_____

green •

white •

6
흰색

7
초록색
_____

purple •

yellow •

8
보라색

B Trace and color.

1

It's red.

2

It's purple.

3

It's green.

4

It's orange.

5

It's yellow.

6

It's black.

Let's Talk

A Check and write.

1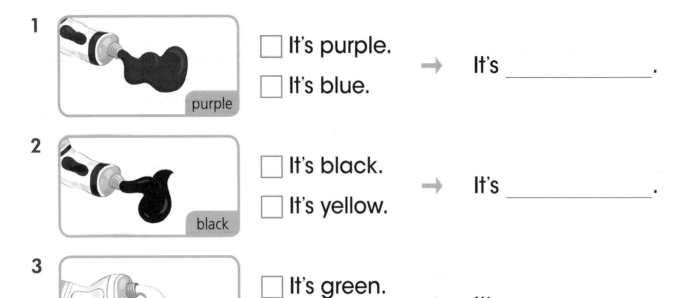

purple

- [ ] It's purple.
- [ ] It's blue.

→ It's _____.

2

black

- [ ] It's black.
- [ ] It's yellow.

→ It's _____.

3

white

- [ ] It's green.
- [ ] It's white.

→ It's _____.

B Follow and color.

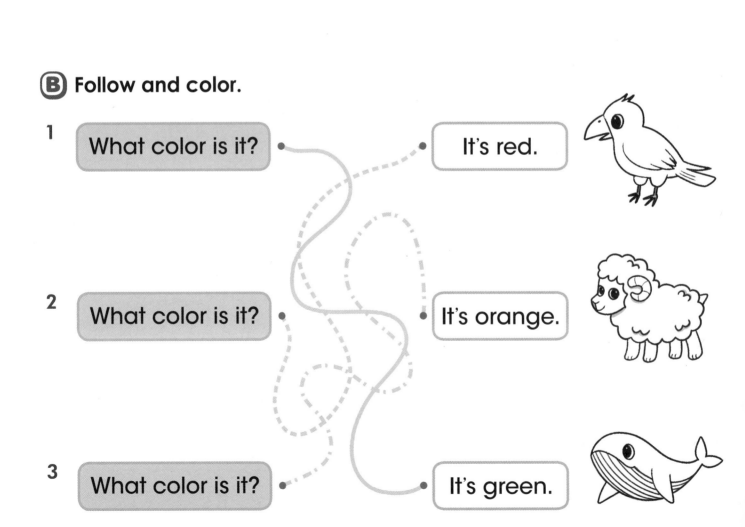

1 What color is it? — It's red.

2 What color is it? — It's orange.

3 What color is it? — It's green.

Words

Ⓐ Look and write.

red	blue	green	yellow
purple	orange	black	white

1

노란색
_____

2

파란색
_____

3

주황색
_____

4

빨간색
_____

5

검은색
_____

6

초록색
_____

7

흰색
_____

8

보라색
_____

Subject Link

(A) Look, read, and circle.

1

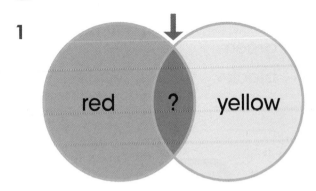

A: What color is it?

B: It's (white / orange).

2

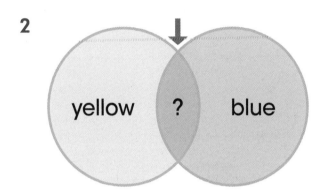

A: What color is it?

B: It's (green / black).

(B) What color comes next? Color and write.

1

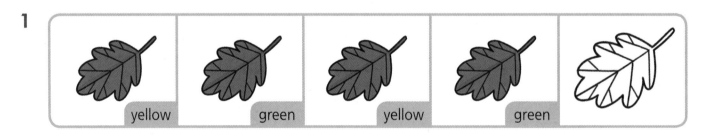

It's y_____.

2

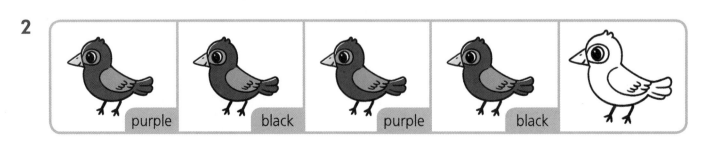

It's p_____.

Phonics

Ⓐ Look, match, and write.

1.  k •
   j •
   • ite _____

2.  j •
   l •
   • ion _____

3.  j •
   k •
   • am _____

4.  k •
   l •
   • ing _____

5.  j •
   l •
   • emon _____

6.  k •
   j •
   • eep _____

What Shape Is It?

Learn

A Trace and circle.

1 **circle**

2 **star**

3 **heart**

4 **square**

5 **triangle**

6 **rectangle**

7 **diamond**

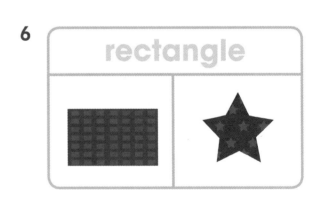

B Draw and circle.

1

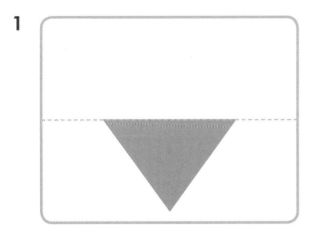

It's a (diamond / star).

2

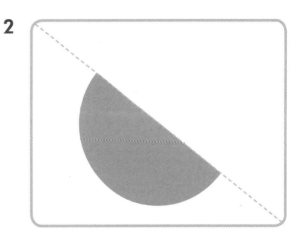

It's a (rectangle / circle).

3

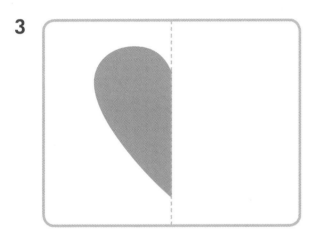

It's a (square / heart).

4

It's a (star / triangle).

5

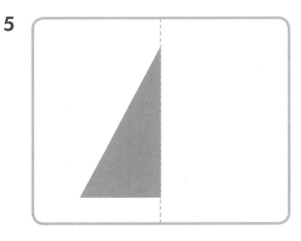

It's a (triangle / circle).

6

It's a (square / heart).

Let's Talk

A Circle and write.

1

rectangle

heart

It's a _____ .

2

star

diamond

It's a _____ .

3

circle

square

It's a _____ .

4

diamond

triangle

It's a _____ .

B What shape comes next? Draw and check.

1

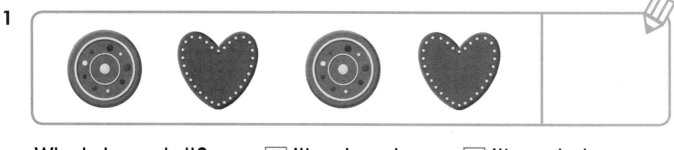

What shape is it? ☐ It's a heart. ☐ It's a circle.

2

What shape is it? ☐ It's a square. ☐ It's a star.

Words

A Find, circle, and write.

1   b k c i r c l e l a

    _____

2   s t a s t a r d s e

    _____

3   g n t r i a n g l e

    _____

4   d i a m o n d b a o

    _____

5   p s q u a r e e s p

    _____

6   l r e c t a n g l e

    _____

7   f y t h h e a r t k

    _____

Subject Link

A Look and number.

1　2　3　4

☐ It's a circle.

☐ It's a diamond.

☐ It's a square.

☐ It's a rectangle.

B Connect and write.

star	triangle

1

A: What shape is it?

B: It's a _____.

2

A: What shape is it?

B: It's a _____.

Phonics

A Look and write.

1

☐ x

2

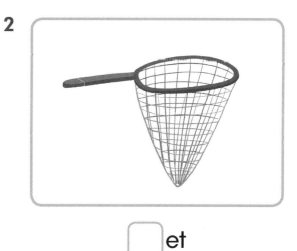

☐ et

3

☐ oon

4

☐ ine

5

☐ onkey

6

☐ ctopus

It's a Red Pen

Learn

Ⓐ Look and match.

1  • • book • • ⓐ

2  • • watch • • ⓑ

3  • • ball •  • ⓒ

4  • • umbrella •  • ⓓ

5  • • pencil •  • ⓔ

6  • • bag •  • ⓕ

7  • • pen • • ⓖ

8  • • crayon • • ⓗ

B Match and trace.

1. It's | a red • — • pencil.

2. It's | a blue • — • ball.

3. It's | a green • — • crayon.

4. It's | a yellow • — • book.

5. It's | a black • — • watch.

6. It's | a purple • — • pen.

Let's Talk

A Read and circle.

1

It's a blue [watch] / [pen].

2

It's a yellow [crayon] / [bag].

3

It's a purple [book] / [umbrella].

4

It's a red [pencil] / [ball].

B Read, choose, and color.

1 It's a red pen.

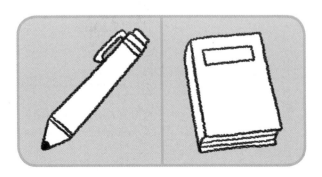

2 It's a black crayon.

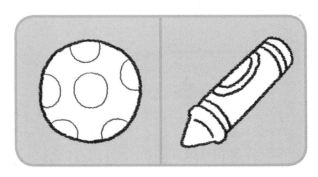

Words

A Circle and write.

1
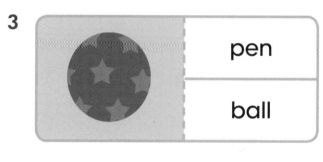
bag

watch

It's a blue _____.

2

umbrella

crayon

It's a yellow _____.

3

pen

ball

It's a red _____.

4

book

pencil

It's a green _____.

5

watch

book

It's an orange _____.

6
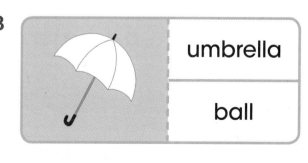
crayon

pen

It's a black _____.

7
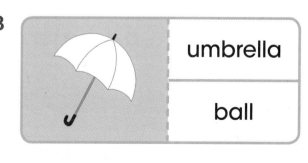
bag

pencil

It's a purple _____.

8
umbrella

ball

It's a white _____.

Subject Link

A Match and color.

1 | It's a red bag. | •

•ⓐ

2 | It's a blue watch. | •

•ⓑ

3 | It's a green crayon. | •

•ⓒ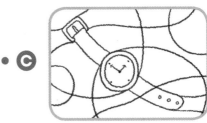

B Find, circle, and write.

1 **b d a p e n l k** → It's a yellow _____.

2 **b o p a j b a l l z** → It's a white _____.

3  **d e h b o o k t** → It's a purple _____.

Phonics

A Circle and write.

1

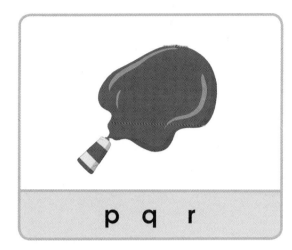

p q r

_____ed

2

p q r

_____ig

3

p q r

_____en

4

p q r

_____uilt

5

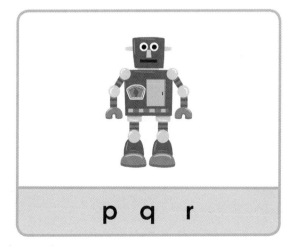

p q r

_____obot

6

p q r

_____ueen

UNIT 7 This Is My Family

Learn

A Trace and number.

1 dad	**2** sister	**3** grandpa	**4** uncle
5 mom	**6** grandma	**7** aunt	**8** brother

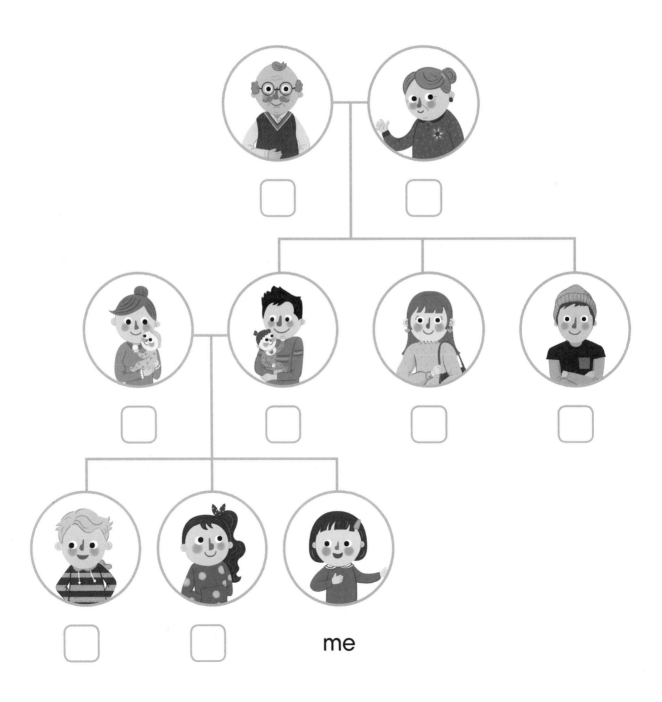

me

B **Read and match.**

1 This is my grandpa. •   • **a**

2 This is my grandma. •   • **b**

3 This is my dad. •   • **c**

4 This is my mom. •   • **d**

5 This is my brother. •   • **e**

6 This is my sister. •   • **f**

Let's Talk

Ⓐ Read and number.

This is my dad. ☐

This is my sister. ☐

This is my brother. ☐

This is my mom. ☐

Ⓑ Circle and write.

1

This is my _____.
(aunt / uncle)

2

This is my _____.
(grandma / grandpa)

3

This is my _____.
(dad / aunt)

Words

A Look and unscramble.

1
agnradp
_____

2
armndag
_____

3
dda
_____

4
mmo
_____

5
tnau
_____

6
eclun
_____

7
rthorbe
_____

8
rstsie
_____

Subject Link

(A) Read and check.

1

- ☐ This is my grandpa.
- ☐ This is my aunt.

2

- ☐ This is my uncle.
- ☐ This is my mom.

3

- ☐ This is my grandma.
- ☐ This is my brother.

4

- ☐ This is my uncle.
- ☐ This is my sister.

(B) Read and choose.

1

This is my dad.

2

This is my sister.

Phonics

A Match and write.

1

___ un

2

___ an

3

___ est

4

___ mbrella

5

___ en

6

___ ister

7

___ ncle

8

___ op

I Like Cake

Learn

Ⓐ Trace and number.

cake ☐   cheese ☐   pizza ☐

bread ☐   chicken ☐   ice cream ☐

juice ☐   milk ☐

B Read and match.

1 I like bread.

2 I like cheese.

3 I like cake.

4 I like milk.

5 I like chicken.

6 I like ice cream.

a

b

c

d

e

f

Let's Talk

(A) Circle and write.

1. I like milk / bread . → I like _____ .

2. I like pizza / juice . → I like _____ .

3. I like cake / cheese . → I like _____ .

4. I like chicken / ice cream . → I like _____ .

(B) Read and check.

1. ☐ I like juice.
   ☐ I like cake.

2. ☐ I like chicken.
   ☐ I like bread.

Words

A Read and circle.

1
pizza

2
milk

3
bread

4
cheese

5
chicken

6
ice cream

7
juice

8
cake

Subject Link

(A) Look and match.

1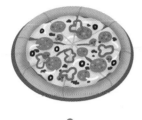

2

3

| I like ice cream. | I like cake. | I like pizza. |

(B) Look and write.

juice   chicken   bread

1

I like _____.

2

I like _____.

3

I like _____.

66

Phonics

(A) Which is different? Look and choose.

1

w

a	b	c
___ eb	___ at	___ atch

2

x

a	b	c
re___	fo___	si___

3

y

a	b	c
___ ellow	___ o-yo	___ pple

4

z

a	b	c
___ oo	___ ite	___ ebra